BEYOND THE BYGONE: WHEN THE PAST PRESENTS THE FUTURE

Nadakkavu, Kozhikode, Kerala, 673011
www.insightpublica.com
e-mail: insightpublica@gmail.com
Title:
Beyond the Bygone: When the Past Presents the Future
Author: **Safna Shabab**
First Edition: October 2024
All rights reserved.
Printed and Published by
InsightinPublica Printers & Publishers Pvt. Ltd.
ISBN 978-93-5517-680-6

BEYOND THE BYGONE: WHEN THE PAST PRESENTS THE FUTURE

SAFNA SHABAB

Description of the Book

This collection of poems reflects the idea of self-discovery which portrays raw emotions. The poems revolve around dreams, aspirations, hope, love, and loss, which dive deep into human experiences. The book speaks about the plight of a young girl who is passionate about following her dreams. I am sure as you delve into the poems, you are going to meet a piece of yourself.

About the Author

Safna is a young poet hailing from Kerala, who is a BBA graduate from Rajagiri College and now she is pursuing law degree. Her ardent desire to write made her a poet. She has a great vision on her life woven the true essence of a human experience through her poems. Amidst the chaos she never failed to run after her dreams. She found solace in writing poems. The book Beyond the Bygone is their self portrait inviting readers to reflect on the past and embrace the present. Through which she tries to convey that 'you are the creator of your own destiny'!

Acknowledgments

I am deeply grateful to my family and friends for their unwavering support and encouragement throughout the journey of creating this poetry collection. You were my light on the darkest days, guiding me and believing in my words even when I doubted myself. Your insistence that I keep writing has been invaluable. To all the writers whose words never failed to inspire me, thank you for igniting the spark of creativity within me. A special thanks to my sister Shabanu Fathima who has been a great companion on this journey -a keen critic and my constant source of motivation. To my best friend Ameena, your belief in me from the very beginning means more than words can express. I also extend my heartfelt gratitude to my favourite teacher Anila Miss for being a steady supporter along the way. To my dear friends Aabi and Archana, thank you for loving me when I forgot to love myself. Your kindness and friendship have been a great comfort. Lastly, to those who have gifted me bitter experiences --thank you. You planted the seeds of rage and heartache that have blossomed into the poems.

I would like to extend my deepest gratitude to Ashitha Ma'am, whose insightful feedback and careful proofreading helped refine this book.

Dedication

Dedicated to my parents, whose belief in my dreams was even stronger than my own. And to all of you who are in a scuttle to achieve your dreams—this book is for you.

Message for readers

I am truly honored to share my story with you and I hope my words find a place in your heart. This book aims to weave a connection between your purpose in life and your passions. My hope is that it sparks a bit of inspiration within you. Beyond telling the story of a young woman striving towards her dreams, this book delves deep into the significance of emotions and self awareness. Remember, we are all unique in our journeys, and our stories reflect that individuality. Beyond the Bygone holds the unspoken emotions that connect us all. This is a gentle reminder that you are loved, and your story matter. May my book be a quiet reflection of your own life in some way. Thank you for joining me on this journey. I deeply appreciate the time you've taken to read my book, and I hope it resonates with you in meaningful ways.

CONTENTS

Beyond the Bygone

Beyond the Bygone

Fuel to My Poem

Unwelcome it was!
Broke into my peace
Shattered I was, struggling to move with ease!
Upended my life, elapsed along
depressive episodes. Thereby,
I scoured into a world where
dark clouds of grief enfolded
my sky, and the droplets of tears
wet my pillows! With leaden steps
I fumbled along, biding by an opened door!

I heard echoes resonating
inside my void heart!
The pain began eroding my
scars, depicting the mark
of my survival! Spilling the
tears of loss, I found myself!

By embracing the darkness
around me, I found my solace!
I forgot about the fathoms of the
sea and the waves that swept my shore,
I drowned! I decided to live my life
before the strange chapter that life
has unfurled before me!
Let my silence speak louder than
the words I chanted!

Beyond the Bygone

Afar from Fiction

I was a girl flitting daintily in my
parents' dreams! Wearing a short white
frock knitted by mom and holding a bear
gifted by dad, I dazzled in the yard!
The black sky adorned in pearls marveled at
me, I was contented by the zephyr,
shoved by the slavering sea, the shooting
star coaxed me to hold my longings.
I never felt alone on the sprawled
shore; the long wait for heavy rain never
made me tired, no love blemished me!!
The life I forged out of fictions was
far away from me!!
I ruminated, staring at my old snaps.

Beyond the Bygone

Woven Threads of Life

From the time you sprouted, the roots of
artistry crept through your veins, making them bleed
poetry! You lie, lie beneath the shade of
words woven into a beautiful limerick!
You fumble through each space of it to ensconce your
flaws, which mirror a gifted poet!
You weave your grief, adorn it on your neck,
and its radiance reflects on your wounded
lips, bearing the weight until your chest chokes!
I write, write about the things that douse my
peace, that shunt my happiness, and those
that fade my smile, followed by grace and success.
My poem mirrors my life, a time machine of emotions untold!

Beyond the Bygone

Thank You

For the rain that has stopped raining, for the
unrequited love that braided a
beautiful sonnet, for the tears that effaced
the grief of my soul, for the waves that washed
the grief from my shore, for the verses that
ensconced a poet,
And for the sea that carries my tales—
Thank you for all that prevails!

Beyond the Bygone

Bloom Where You Are Planted

Everything seems to move around in a
transpose now.
Ink-flinched to spread on the white
paper,words seem like gulped inside and
wounded lips fervouring to spell it.
Of all the tears I have shed and all the
darkest days that crawled through , I found a
girl who has a thousand bizarre dreams!
Amidst all the chaos i was bound to exist
I found a girl who had a clear vision on her life !
The tales that delineated a lonesome soul
among the crowd I found a fighter !
Between all the scars i tried to hide,
I found a woman who marked her existence!
Beyond the smile that i wore as a veil,
I found a girl who was wrapped in mystery !
In my silence I heard a woman shouts
against the unheard voice!

Beyond the Bygone

A Love So Deep

What you are to me cannot be rendered with
words that knit a sonnet embellished with
metaphors!
Your beauty cannot be confined to a
piece of paper; no pen can portray you
fully! You are an ocean that I
cannot gauge the depth of.
You are among the celestial stars that I failed to count.
You are the moon that manifests wherever I go.
You are the autumn that makes my leaves fall.
You are the fiery fire that sparks my tired soul.
You are the comet I wish upon.
You are the twilight that lingered through that awful
day!

Beyond the Bygone

The Spirit of Dreams

I am one among the stars upon the lonely sky,
yet so bright.
Find me woven between the
phrases of my verses; I sew wings
on my scarred skin to buckle
down the spirit of my dreams!
I bury my cries in the tomb of anticipation,
hoping one day they will be heard!
I suture the bruises on my brown skin with a
string of hope, seeking their dissipation!
I adorn the veil of elation on my wounded lips,
wishing one day it will blossom on its own!
And I find asylum amidst the pain,
embracing the whole of me.

Beyond the Bygone

Beneath the Bare Sky

What if time forgot to mount
you inside my head and heart?
Or effaced the memory of you
from the tapestry that once adorned
and hung on my chest?

Over your brown eyes,
I started portraying perceptions of
life afar from my aspect!
There I saw flowers blooming, stars
lining the lonely moon, and falls
that enchanted me unknowingly!
I painted my bare sky with your sacred arms,
which stretched out to hold me in times of despair!
But you left a barren space inside
me when you severed me along
the deep ocean of memories.
What remained were cinders of
poems and a broken heart!

Shall we meet once again,
once again in the haven of love?
So that we can weave a better love story!

Beyond the Bygone

Beyond the Bygone

Whilst the Introspection

It was stillness all around,
the city was in a hustle where
wobbling for something
unreciprocated and uncertain.
The moonlight divested the clouds
and granted pace for her longings.
Autumn sprouted outside the tropics,
nights prolonged, allowing her to
de-stuff the griefs, to hide her
scars, and to listen to her
bellowing voice!

Beyond the Bygone

Oh Rainbow !

Oh Rainbow!
I am bewildered by the solitude of my existence.
Metaphors and syllables are jaded by the
stale verses of lonesomeness and remorse!

Each midnight I scrawled through the pain
I endured in the past and noviced into a
melancholic strain! My poem mourns that I
forgot about my happy tide.

Yes, there was a person that my verses
forgot to reminisce about,
a girl who admired her longings
more than anything in the universe,
a girl who listened to the cryptic
silence of twilight, a girl who
stayed beneath the lonely moon,
who wore a pretty smile
on her face always, who was
wrapped in love, who was
an adjunct and a metonym
of fondness in his sonnet!
Oh Rainbow,
She is now one amid the colours in you.

Beyond the Bygone

The Girl with Colored Insights

She was the girl with coloured
insights that unfurled on her
blank sky. She was trying to
paint her dreams onto it.
Her eyes gleamed in
the dawn of longings
with a blooming
smile on her lips.
Adorned on her head was
a crown of her own beliefs.
So sensitive her heart was,
though it held many.
I remember the day
she flung her dreams away.
Eventually, I saw her soul
dissolving in the faded gray sky.
Never found her smiling again; her
pale face made me weep inside!
Her beautiful body was carved with
scars; I heard her cry, painful it was.
I found her in a corner of a dark room
that echoed her bellowing silence!
Fading memories of bonds that
once held her tight made her insane!
I believe one day she will ascend
to the throne of her own destiny,
with hope her departing part...

Beyond the Bygone

Beyond the Bygone

The Silent Melancholy of Longings

You were once a hope that tied me
to the wantonly moving life of mine!,
a light that guided me to the path
that life has unfurled in front of
the chaotic me! Suddenly you felt
like a Christmas Rose that had
withered before the autumn!
You left me in the midst of love that
bloomed out of my heart and head!
I wonder everything moved fast, time,
seasons, and you, but what makes me
insist on narrating stories and
composing poems about you?
You make me feel everything poetic !
The wind that whirled my curtain,
the sunrays that escape through
my lunette , the dawn that makes
silhouette, the flowers and leaves
that dance to the rhythm of rain,
the gleaming beauty of the sun
that steep down the sea,
the ballad of acoustic waves,
the stars and the moon that abreast
the lonely sky ! Everything
You made me see the beauty
of the bygone and the pain of
the withered!

Beyond the Bygone

 Beyond the Bygone

Dreams Intertwined

A dream emerged from nowhere but
sparked with inspiration, it clung
to my heart when I was about to quit.
Unbidden, it grew alongside my steps,
blind I am, yet clear about my visions and dreams.
I haven't yet loved myself for a
hundred reasons, but this sole
dream is the cause of my selfless love.
Amidst the starry sky, my dream
shines the brightest, a beacon to a
hopeful tomorrow.
It's so near, yet so far.
I tried holding it with my arms,
but it glided along. Then I tried
embracing it with my whole heart,
and it adhered to my being.
See me flying to the
throne of my destiny!

Beyond the Bygone

Apart from Being a Human

I don't mean mere survival in this sphere,
I long to remain a mark of a trail on the shore I belong to!
I don't mean to be a star after my death's
veil, as they said it shines the brightest!
I don't mean to be a dried rose among the old
pages of autographs!
I don't mean to be a person so forgotten, yet
remembered by the tapestry hung on your walls!
But rather a being, living in the cadence of her verses!
Breathing life into words, etching moments in time!

                    Beyond the Bygone

A Girl Once a Rainbow

Afar from a being whose
sufferings were painted with
crimson upon her bare sky,
she had been a rainbow!
Her tale was different, so was she;
her journey was difficult, so were her words.
She was a floss woven
and known for her courage!
Apart from a poet, she was nothing
but a cinder of memories,
a canvas with hues of the pain she bore,
a veil for the scars that remained
on her brown skin, and a woman
who resided in her solace!

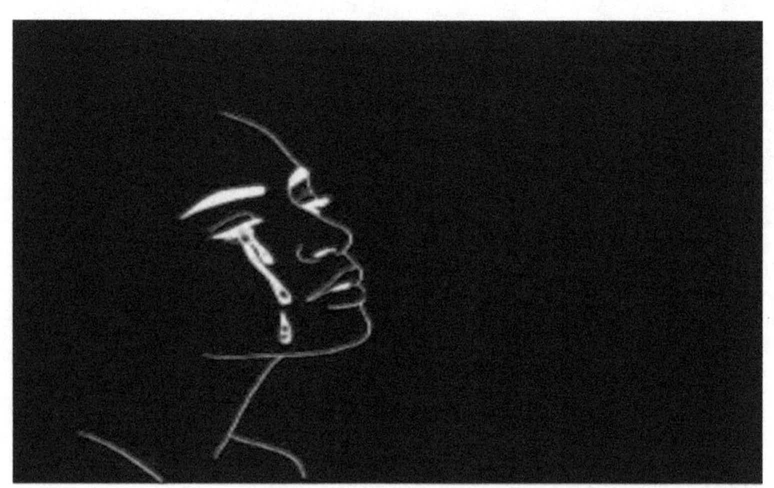

Beyond the Bygone

I Bleed Poetry

It took me ages to discern
that poetry voiced my emotions!
See, words surmount the lexicons and spill art!
An art that caressed my soul,
which stood beside me to hold off
the shore that deluded my way!
Thereupon, I knuckled under the
home in between the lines of my verses.
There, I found love sprawling,
grief resting, and malice burning!

Beyond the Bygone

Birth of a New Hope

Dandelions unfurled in
the pasture of my dreams,
stars shone the brightest
of all nights in my sky.
The aura of stardust braced,
entwined in magic, as she
danced with grace, beneath
the illuminating moon!

The wind of the transition
swirled the curtain of my life's
window, making me testify to a
new world where dreams take flight
and reality blends with whispers of night!

Beyond the Bygone

Echoes of Pain

She is the girl who
descends between each
phrase of her poem to
destuff the burdens, and who
fumbles each space to
weave her longings that
are effused and tangled in
her barest dreams!
Intertwined Echoes
In twilight's embrace, she
finds solace within
whispers of forgotten stars,
unraveling tales of her
heart's journey!

Beyond the Bygone

Under the Shade of Verses

Her poems are the
clamouring of her silence,
on which she hid the
love that dissipated
from her, dusted the
bygone reminiscence,
delineated the sunsets
that obscured, portrayed
the faces that were
secluded, diffused the
pain she endured!
Metaphors dance upon
her page,
emotions in the symphony,
cascading rage,
in the freedom of her verse.

Beyond the Bygone

Solace Amidst the Pain

On the hush of a winter night,
when petunia blossomed,
I felt a slice of my life in my arms.
I cradle you, my little one!
I clamped you to my heart and
my throb sang you to sleep!
You were enveloped in magic
that vanished my deep despair!
Your gaze, a love so pure,
I am captivated by your tender grace!
Your smile was a beacon
that forever lies inside!
Your arms are so white, yet so delicate,
nestled on my scars,
I never felt the pain!
Your footsteps were
louder than the bellowing
voice inside, making it becalm!
It too was the birth of a new mom
who abided a decade for that
smile abreast the lonely sky!

Beyond the Bygone

The Melancholy of Rain

It was on one fine evening,
raining heavily outside.
I peeped through the half
opened window of my room.
I was half asleep.
The petrichor pervaded inside.
I awoke. It was cloudy.
I listened to the birds screeching
and racing for shelter,
it was a calm rain, but it
reminded me of a bygone love,
unabated malice, the circumstances
that infuriated me, the crowd that
alienated me, that lonely 17-year-old
inside the four walls of her
bedroom in tears, that 21-year-old
surrounded by the thousand and hundred
books which witnessed each drop
from her eyes, that girl who dreamt
of colourful tomorrows, the girl who
longed for a twilight without
crying to bed, the girl who
fumbles with her longings within
the lines of her sonnet,
it reminds me of myself, who still
battles with her inner demons.

Beyond the Bygone

Roots of Resilience

Growing into a wild verse, the roots of
shattered dreams hinge on my head!
Mortal thoughts took birth from
the womb of a catastrophe!
The more I started evading,
the more it pervaded!
Nourished by my cries and
screams, it grew over my soul!
Like a leaf in autumn,
my smile started fading!
The roots of my shattered
dreams crept up until then,
and I resisted the storm!
And yet I arose like a phoenix
from the captivating flame,
bloomed amidst the mud I was planted.
Let my words that outpoured
mound a deep sense of
longings and belongings!
I hesitate to let it grow and
buried it in the crematorium,
For it sleeps under the
warmth of my heart!

Beyond the Bygone

                    Beyond the Bygone

The Weight of Absence

Beneath the dark sky,
heavy with the grief of separation, poured
the droplets of tears from heaven!
Demented I was, screeched
for a presence disappeared!
The dried petals of chrysanthemum
unfurled, the smell of her
old clothes pervaded my soul!
Darkness all around, I fumbled
to hold her hand, I dropped off!
Bestow me with one more
chance to hold her close!
Just one more turn to lie on
her lap, gazing at the starry sky,
to fill up the void that
echoes her memories!
Dear grandma, I hope we will meet
on the other side of destiny,
where life is immortal!
Will dead people own a room in our heart?
Or do we ourselves lock them inside?
The most sensitive question
I have ever encountered!

Beyond the Bygone

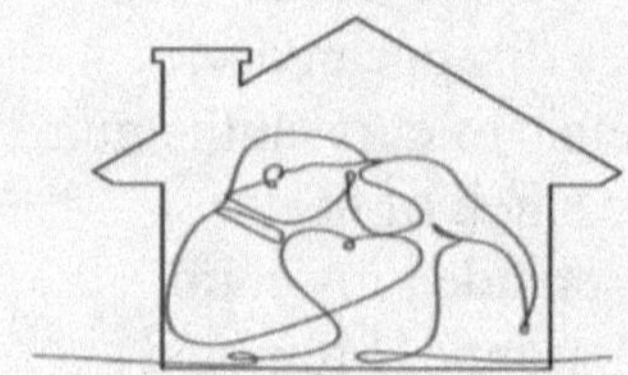

Beyond the Bygone

Home

Together we will create a home
with no shouts and anger,
peace all around the corners,
a new beginning of joy divests the
curtain of grief and remorse.
Sun rays intrude through the
half-opened window and make
a canopy of new hope,
Seeing each other's grinning
faces, we wake up and dance
in the shower!
We fix the shattered pieces of us,
and embellish the scars that
overreach the skin, not our heart.
We have different stories and
we got through and bore a
varied fathom of pain, but
still we make a safe home in
each other's arms!

Beyond the Bygone

Remember Me

Do you remember the tune
I draped in love for you?
Do you recall the shade
I unfurled in the pasture where
you bled, holding the flag,
and leading thousands of combatants
yelling for welfare amidst the chaos?
Remember those splendid
eyes that ensconced love?

Remember the prayers
recited by hearts you missed?
Remember the palm that
fondled you in the darkest of
days and still resists to
portray the beauty of you?
One day you will realise that
it was all about you when
those words, touches, and songs
go to the bareness!
Hold my palm, and you will
know my life that is immersed
in your thoughts!

Beyond the Bygone

The Home I Cherish

I see my future in your ardent eyes,
I can see our children hauling your beard,
Clinging to your shoulders, resisting you to move, and
you fondling them gently,
your overjoyed face when you
get hold of the newborn!
I can see the happy me
and you sitting on a couch, spending
a rainy evening with hot coffee!
I can see us being busy in the
kitchen preparing dinner!
I can see us lying in bed on a
Sunday afternoon with tangled
hands and messy hair!
I can see me loving myself
a bit more through you!
I can see your contented face
with a grin, aloof from the corridor!

 Beyond the Bygone

The Snippets of My Journey

All of my poems are the
snippets of stale memories,
whining of cryptic love that
unveils through the metaphors
of my verses, the pain endured,
the sullen picture of friendship that
was a family once, the tale of
bygone love, the metaphors that
acclaimed the love that
I never had, the beauty of the
dawn that peeps through my window,
the midnight that longs for the beloved,
the stars and the moon that
embellish the lonely sky,
the rain that pours upon the holy Earth,
the elation while wishing at the dog star!
How beautiful it is to feel
things through mere words!

Beyond the Bygone

You!

There are days when everything
seems obscured, obscured by
the suffocation of a frothy past,
hazy tomorrows, a war between
paradoxical thoughts in me.
There are days when my heart
longs for a delusional love!
Some days feel like everything
detours away from my control…
Even though there are specks
of hope in each day to
long for tomorrows.
I still recall the day the moon
shone too bright and awoke
me till dawn thinking about you!
It was just you and me,
I still remember. You made me
romanticize the dark nights and
bright streets, tangled hands,
and the rhythm of rain that matches
our love song! If your love were an
ocean, I would have dove so deep.

Beyond the Bygone

A Soul's Revival

When my eyes gazed at yours,
A blaze of serenity rippled across my face!
I beheld the dazzling rain around,
Embellishing the warmth of your love!
The fragrance of sweet alyssum unfurled
In the pasture and bowed my mind,
Descending into the
disarming smile of you!
Autumn never dreaded my falling
When I found your hands to hold me!

You wove out a ceaseless
ballad of your love
That still echoes in my empty heart!!

Beyond the Bygone

The Heart that Dissolved

You loved my scars when
everyone kept on twinging them.
You embraced me in your
arms, knowing I was stone dead
inside. You painted my scrawled
soul with the radiant hue of your
lips.
You adorned the dark
nights that horrify me
with celestial stars! You
heard the bellowing
voice inside when everyone
slandered my silence. You
clenched my frigid palm
like I couldn't haul
my fingers tangled with yours.
You planted my heart in you,
which slowly dissolved in yours!

Beyond the Bygone

Whispers of the Sea

I retraced the days that passed by,
I probed yesterdays.
When did I fling the dreams
that clung to my chest?
When did the cold zephyr of
bonds break apart?
When did the novelty of
twilight become stale?
Why did the beauty of dawn
baffle me?
What towed my psyche to hysterical
and dumbed my thoughts?
Why does time reminisce about
the broken past again?
When did the black beckon me?
Why did the slavering sea make me
lonely on that unfurled shore?
Why did my wandering soul crave
an unrequited love?
Why do the cryptic silences of
the facts that I schlepped on my chest
resonate inside my head?
Why do the songs I fondle fail to
remember your name?
Why is my heart throbbing
and unfolding tears?
Why does my poem sing
a melancholic strain?

Beyond the Bygone

A Piece of Me

Like a shattered shard of a star,
she beamed beneath the sky by
reflecting the lonely moon
and made the canopy brighter!

 Beyond the Bygone

Whether Love Deserves a Second Chance ?

Bestow me with one more turn,
To give back the love I connived once,
To suture the wounds befall by
unreturned emotions, and to heal my
scars that marked the wreck of grief,
 To gaze at the sky till dawn,
to count the remaining stars and
those ineffable stories of you that
I absconded behind the strung
words embellished by the metaphors!
To outright that ceaseless
poetry that portrays your beauty..
To walk together in the rain
that keeps up all the night And
To dream a little longer and
to love a little deeper !!!

Beyond the Bygone

Corridors

When I ruminate over the
old photographs,
Memories slow down,
reviving the past, fretting it
with a fleck of smile on my face!
That black-and-white snap ink
honouring the beauty of the days
we spent, when we were
wearing our blue-and-white
school uniform with black hijab, and
you with goggles!
I still remember the days
we laughed together, the days we
became a shade for each other,
the days we coloured our gray sky
with hues of our dreams!
It took me to the days when we
used to stand on the veranda of
the school when the sky turned dark,
holding our hands and you narrating
your bygone love story and making
me weave poetry out of it....

    Beyond the Bygone

Ode to My Eternal Muse

For you, I can be a fiery fire
that sparkles your soul.
For you, I can be the rain of love
to quicken your withered leaves.
For you, I can be a tide to wash
away all your sorrows!
For you!
For you, I can be the sun
to lighten up your day.
For you, I can be the moon
and stars to adorn your dark sky!
For you,
I can knit a ceaseless ballad of love…
You are an endless sonnet, beloved,
that cannot be quelled in a few stanzas!

Beyond the Bygone

Once Again

I wish I could find you once again
betwixt the lines of my verses,
in the middle of the old
pages of my journal,
among the words
I scribbled and from the tales
I knitted.

Our eyes will meet again
in the middle of twilight,
where cosmic bodies brighten up
and narrate their cosmic
love, and there we will stare at
each other, not wanting to leave.

I hope we will weave a different
story the next time we meet,
which is chaste and pure.
A love that heals and
kisses my scar, a love that
never makes me feel alone.

I will stare at you a bit longer
until my eyes rest.

Beyond the Bygone

The Beauty of Unwritten

I hope one day you will be living
a life that you dream of having,
a day will come when those
unabated malice no longer stab you,
a day will come
when you can affirm a love
that never deceives you,
a day will come when you never get
tired of that unbidden love,
you laugh till your tummy
aches, that earnest smile,
when the midnight longs
for you to dream of a dawn
where you can arise seeing
his hand weave with yours,
when you realize all the
spasms you endured craft
a beautiful verse of life.

Beyond the Bygone

A Letter to Your Aching Self

This is to your aching self…

Whose thoughts are muddled around, who's anxious over the tomorrows, who awakes each night longing for an unrequited love, whose eyes are overflowing with tears of echoing memories, who looks up at the sky seeing nothing but the darkness, who can't flatter the beauty of dawn, the moonlight that knocks on the door of longings, the wind that gusts the curtains, the smell of rain—everything… I know it's hard for you to bear. I know romanticizing the emptiness over mere words cannot heal your scars. I am not here to shuffle the trauma you went through!

Fight until you bow the knee to your fortitude! Make yourself proud, but not in the sense that you should be completely perfect, as we all have limitations that we refuse to accept at times. Disappointments start from there. I know it's hard to get up and heal the scars forthwith. But try. I can't see anything hard about you. You are not wounded; you have gotten abilities that make you unique. I see no problems that you can't solve. I can't see any challenges beyond your ability.

You are confined to a narrow world where everything seems abnormal. Your emotions are valid.

One thing I can do is write. Write about everything you are going through and assure you that you are worthy enough to be happy. Smile. Smile like you are the happiest person in the world.

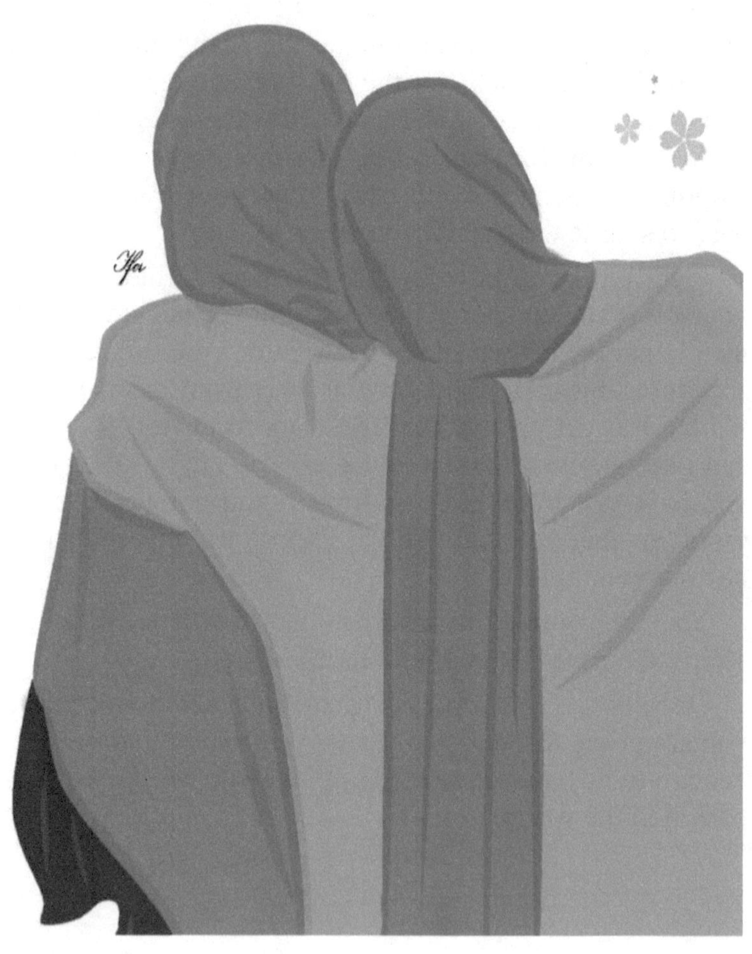

Beyond the Bygone

Dear Aabi

In the realm where everyone is entwined in bogus love,
I was destined to find a true friend,
who fills the chasm of my mysterious silence.
A girl who is wrapped in magic, bound by stardust. She
came into my being with a helping hand!
There I was drowning deep in the sea of despair, suffo
cated. I was reckless about what was happening around!
I found her arms extending towards me; holding me, we
walked together to the throne of hope!
She made me realise that no light enters through a closed
door; for it, it has to be broken!
She arranged the pieces of me and grafted a soul who
regained the power to move forward!
Thank you for your existence, for being beside me when
I could see nothing but darkness!
And thank you for figuring out the puzzle that life ufurled
in front of the clueless me!

Beyond the Bygone

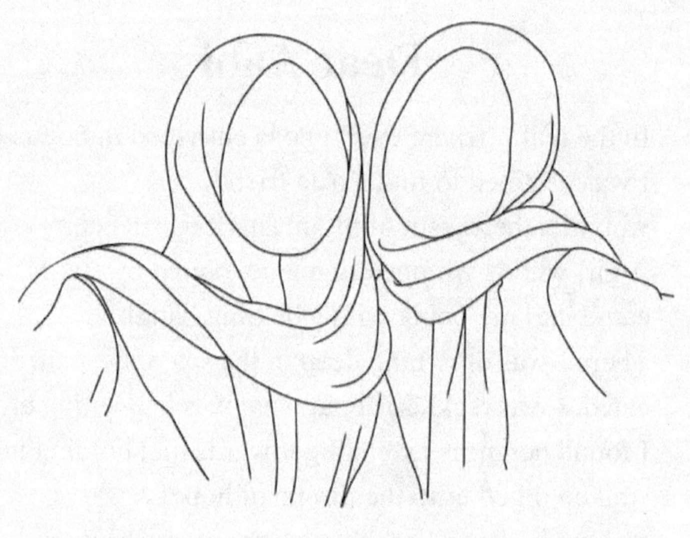

Beyond the Bygone

Thank you Amy

When the dark clouds muffled my sky, was
about to rain I found you slaked my land
and ease my heart!
When it obscured myself amidst the clouds, you
elicited me as a star so forgotten!
When the pain of separation invaded my being
You awoke with me!
When I was alone on the shore you came
as a wave that hugged my foot so gentle!
You mesmerized me showing the colors of the sky
that shades of life are beautiful in their own way !
When the roots of resilience sought my way you reigned
in the pasture of my veins.

When seasons changed,love blemished, scars loomed
the skin , malice eroded the head and heart, regrets accreted
between the chest resisting to exhale the voice,

Words that outpoured faltered fervouring a bygone story
,you listened.

My best friend only you heard those bellowing voices!

When the time was slipping away , you gave meaning
to my life

Beyond the Bygone

Echoes of My Heart

Sometimes I wish I could freeze time. Those days when everything was close to my soul, and I don't know when it all changed. Tears are rolling down my cheeks when those reminiscences hit me hard. When I retrospect the paths I crossed, the pain I endured, the lessons I learned, the people I met, the situations I encountered, the love I felt, the bonds I made, and the setbacks I suffered, I realized how powerful I was to face those. But I don't know why I am trying to efface some memories of people who left me, because it is itself neglecting to wash away from my mind. Maybe because those people spawned a bond that proved to be bogus later. But still, I say I miss them, romanticizing those happy days with them just to believe and make others believe that I am not alone, through my verses.

Beyond the Bygone

Before You Become Stories ....

Let your soul find solace in relying on the power ofwords!
Let your pain creep and trail on the branches of your
heart; there it grows, blossoming into bushes of roses.
Let your scars suture with the thread of hope!
Let your pain follow the light of fireflies and move into
the bareness of vulnerability!
Let yourself break your silence and shout out to the world
that you are living, above a mere existence!
Let yourself remain a piece of art that's carved in the
hearts of people!
Let yourself decide your destiny; don't give others a
chance to!
Let success blossom in the pasture of your life.
Before you become stories, let your words weave a
beautiful sonnet portraying a woman so strong.
Beyond the bygone, there is a spark of life that seeks
solace in the cascade of her dreams!
There lies a woman yearning to narrate her
life before the world.
Words, a beacon of her existence so strong.
She wove a beautiful ballad of loss and longing.
Beyond the bygone, there lies a woman who is devoted
to
fixing herself from the ember of despair.
There she found asylum in the branches of her verses.
Let my words be the voice you longed to hear!
Let us all fly, fixing each other's wings.

Beyond the Bygone